I0469491

Waste Not
Want Not

A Bench Jewelers Guide to
Scrap Material Management

By

Brad Simon

Copyrighted 2003
Bench Media LLC

BenchBusiness.com

Table of Contents

Waste Not – Want Not

There is an old saying, "Cleanliness is next to Godliness." I am not sure where this saying originated, certainly not from the Bible! However, when it comes to the jewelry shop, Cleanliness may not be next to Godliness, but it is certainly next to Profits.

A dirty cluttered shop has a detrimental effect on Productivity and Profits.

➤ A stone dropped in a lap tray that is full of tools and filings, or on a floor that has not been swept, will take more time to find.

➤ The chance of a dropped stone hitting a steel tool and chipping is greater.

➤ Small items may become misplaced or lost among the clutter.

➤ Small pieces of gold on the floor from filing, buffing, and other operations in the shop, cling to the bottom of shoes and literally walk out the door of the shop.

➤ Tools kept in the lap tray will accumulate gold dust from filing and grinding operations. From there the gold becomes either lost from wiping on the workers' clothes and towels or carried around the shop on their hands.

This all adds unnecessary expense to the shop. A dirty cluttered shop affects Profits because of the high value of the metal used. When it comes to recovering precious metal, nothing is worthless. However, If you walk into many repair shops you will find jewelers behaving as if it were. Many jewelers do not realize what a valuable asset their scrap is. They have been pleasantly surprised by the amount of additional revenues received from a refiner when a clean and orderly shop is maintained.

To keep your bench clean a procedure needs to be followed. At least once a day clean your lap tray on your bench. At the end of the day, sweep the floor. Do this while the jobs you worked on are in the cleaner. Perform a more complete job once a month. I must emphasize here this is not extra time you need to find, it is time you would spend looking for stones etc., if you did not do the cleaning. It is not spending more time it is just spending the time differently. If your bench and shop are organized and you clean regularly it does not take that much time.

Additional revenues from the refiner are pure profits. No additional time is spent, remember you spend the time either cleaning or looking for items you dropped, there is no additional cost involved. Since you already are sending sweeps to the refiner, it does not cost any more to send the additional sweeps.

Scrap Material Storage

In the jewelry shop, you need to keep five different containers to keep your scrap materials separated. Do not throw an old gold mounting into a container with the polishing waste and filters. You will not receive the full amount of money for that ring. You need to send it in with other mountings. For highest return, you need to keep your scrap separated.

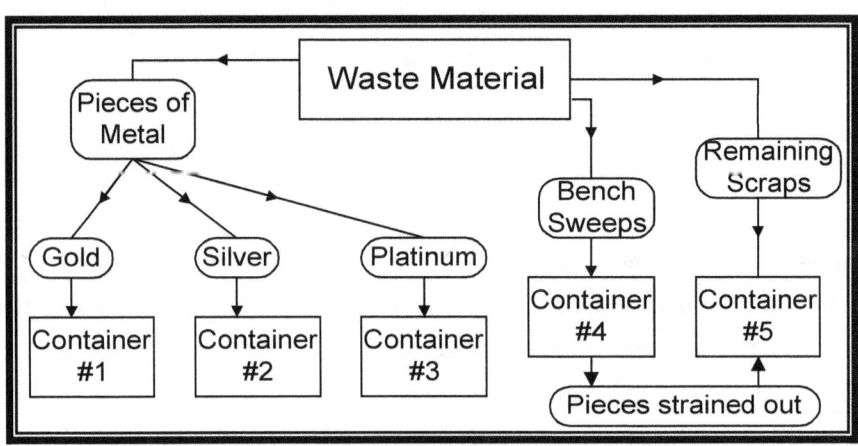

3

Scrap Metal

The first three containers are for pieces of clean metal. This would include anything from old ring mountings to old crowns. Place any piece of metal large enough to pick up with your fingers in these containers. This needs to be clean material. Clean off all dirt and flux or boric acid, before placing into these containers and remove all stones, tags and stickers from the jewelry. These containers are for metal only.

Keep a separate container for Gold, Silver, and Platinum. Depending on the refiner you use, the gold and silver may be combined. Some refiners charge an extra fee to process the silver out of the gold. This makes it worth while to keep these metals separated. Always keep Platinum scrap separate from gold and silver. It is not possible to profitably refine a small amount of platinum out of a large quantity of gold and silver.

These containers are for karat gold, silver, and platinum metals only. Do not contaminate them with gold filled, gold plate, or any base metal jewelry. Place these into container #5 or a separate container for them.

High-Grade Sweeps

The fourth container that you need to keep in the jewelry shop is for high-grade bench sweeps. Some refiners will supply you with a plastic jar with a screw top lid for these sweeps. Any type of container with a wide mouth top can be used; an old coffee can with a plastic lid works well.

In this container, place any sweeps with 50% gold content or higher. The purity of the sweeps is considered here not the purity of the gold. For example: 50% 14k gold filings, and 50% wood and metal filings, grit off sand paper etc. Do not place any broken saw blades in this container or old scraps of emery paper. This is for fairly clean bench sweeps out of your lap tray only.

Low-Grade Sweeps

The fifth container that you need to keep in the shop is for low-grade sweeps. This is to collect anything in the shop, that you have not collected in one of the other four containers. This container needs to be much larger than the others are. A large cardboard drum or box with a plastic liner, so that the dust accumulated is not lost, is ideal for this purpose. In this container place:

➢ Floor Sweeps
➢ Polishing Waste
➢ Vacuum Cleaner Bags
➢ Sink Trap Sludge
➢ Used Emory Paper, Saw Blades
➢ Low-Grade Bench Sweeps

Floor Sweeps

You should sweep the floor of the shop daily and mop monthly. Dump the dirty water from mopping in a sink with a gold trap in the drain. Never dump the water in the toilet or other drain without a trap.

If you have carpet on the floor of the shop, call your refiner for a large drum. Remove the carpet from the floor and send it to the refiner. Use the money you receive to put down a vinyl floor. The money you will accumulate by being able to sweep up debris off the floor makes changing the floor covering worth while. Being able to find small items dropped on the floor that would have been lost in the carpet is an added benefit.

Polishing Waste

You should also place in this container all polishing waste from the polishing machine. This includes the dust and dirt in the machine, old filters, and all the old buffs.

Clean out the polishing machine once a week, including vacuuming off the filter. Always vacuum from the side dirt enters the filter. Never from the other side pulling dirt through the filter. Change the filter every other month.

If dirty air blows out of the polishing machine while using, you have waited too long to clean it out and replace the filter. You can tell if dust accumulates on the wall or around where the air comes out of the dust collector. Changing the filters regularly not only helps profits by accumulating more precious metal dust, but also improves the health of the workers, by not having to breathe all the dust and dirt into their lungs.

In large trade shops and manufacturers, these two items (floor sweeps and polishing waste) are kept separate. However, in the typical retail shop there is not enough of either material accumulated during the year to justify two refining charges.

Vacuum Cleaner

A shop vacuum cleaner is a necessity. As it makes clean up easier, you are likely to do it more often. This vacuum cleaner is for shop use only, and should never be used outside the shop. Vacuum your shop daily. Include the floor, workbenches, bottoms of employee's shoes, clothes, and any other areas that might hold particles of precious metal. Save the bags from the vacuum cleaner in this container.

Sink Trap

Install a special precious metal trap in the drain line on the sink in the shop. There are several styles available from tool suppliers. Be certain to purchase one that is made to trap precious metal particles, not just loose stones. For the retail shop, the small drum trap with a separating screen is adequate. Clean this trap out whenever water slows going down the drain.

To clean out the trap, place a dishpan or similar item under the drain. Remove the trap by unscrewing and dump the contents into the dishpan. Wash out all the sludge in the bottom of the trap. Clean the separating screen thoroughly, if not it will clog prematurely causing you to clean the trap more often.

The content of the dishpan needs to settle and the clean water poured off the top. Swirl the remaining water around in the pan. Use a motion similar to panning gold. As the sludge swirls around in the pan, heavier items will remain on the bottom. Look for any loose stones that may have been trapped in the drain and remove them. Allow the content to settle and pour off as much water as possible. Place all the sludge from the pan into a container to allow the remaining water to evaporate. When the sludge has dried completely place it in the container of low-grade sweeps.

Used Tools

Place all broken saw blades in this container. These should always be collected and not thrown away as fine particles of gold become caught in the teeth and can be refined. Also all old emery paper, burs, bristle brushes, rubber abrasive wheels, anything you use to sand, grind, or polish gold needs to be saved in this container after they are worn out.

Low-Grade Bench Sweeps

Always clean your lap tray and bench before carving waxes, placing your filings in the container of high-grade sweeps. After carving the wax, you need to clean your bench of all the wax filings and place them into the container of low-grade sweeps. Do not throw them away, some gold filings and residue will be swept up from your bench as you clean up the wax. Do not throw this money away, but do not fill the container of high-grade sweeps with a lot of wax.

Preparing for Shipment

When you are ready to send your scraps to the refiner to be processed, sort the container of high-grade sweeps. As you clean up your workspace daily, try to keep the material separated as much as possible. However sometimes items get into the containers that should not be there.

It is easy to sort the container of high-grade scrap by laying a sheet of plastic about two feet square on a work surface. Use a strainer, the type children play with in the sandbox, to sift the material. Take the material out of the container a little at a time and sift it on to the plastic. Place anything that is too large to pass through the strainer into another container of scrap. If it is a piece of metal, such as a shank or crown, place it in the appropriate container. Place pieces of broken saw blades, emery paper, and such, in the container of low-grade scrap.

After sifting through everything in the container, pick up the plastic by the corners and dump the contents back into the can. This is your high-grade scrap ready to send to the refiner.

Clean the items in your scrap metal (containers 1, 2, & 3) for a higher return. Place them in a metal strainer, a 4" to 6" strainer works well. Place the strainer with the metal to be cleaned into the ultrasonic cleaner. Clean all of the dirt, flux, or boric acid off the scrap metal that you have accumulated. The cleaner the scrap, the higher return you will receive from the refiner. The rate of return from the refiner is based on the purity of the material received. If the gold content of the total material received falls too low, the refiner will pay at the lower rate on their chart. Do not spend a lot of time cleaning your scrap. However, removing excessive dirt and flux will be beneficial.

Package your shipment carefully and seal the contents securely. Enclose a packing list stating contents (type of material and weight), instructions, and most importantly your name address and telephone number.

Before sending your material in to be refined always weigh the material. This is for two reasons.

1. The refiner will weigh it upon receipt. If there is a discrepancy, they can notify you of the discrepancy before they begin the refining process.

2. To check your refiners pricing chart. Never send in material to be refined if the weight of your material falls within their minimum charge structure. If you pay the minimum refining charge you are paying the highest price to have your scrap refined. Always accumulate your scrap long enough to get beyond the minimum charge of the refiner.

Refiners vary greatly in the minimum charges they charge and the rate of return they give. You should contact several refiners and receive their pricing chart before deciding upon the refiner to use. Find a refiner whose pricing structure fits with the amount of scrap you have to process. Never Pay A Minimum Refining Charge, if you do you are paying too much to get your scrap refined.

A typical timetable for a retail shop is to send in the low-grade scrap for refining once a year. This could be done around the first of the year after cleaning up the shop from the long Christmas hours. At that time, send in the high-grade scrap as well. Send both packages together with a note to the refiner, stating that you want the two packages refined in the most economical way. Depending upon the size of your lots, they will refine them either together or separately which ever gives you the better return.

Enough high-grade scrap will have been accumulated by the end of the summer to send in a second time by itself. Usually, not enough low-grade scrap is accumulated to send it in more than once a year. This has worked well for many stores. You need to weigh your scrap and decide what timetable would work best for your shop.

Sending in your scrap on a consistent yearly basis has its advantages. You can compare your return from one year to the next to make sure you are getting maximum return on your scrap. By keeping records, you develop a history of your precious metal recovery. This will help you predict what your returns should be, and investigate any major variations.

Settlement

To maximize the profits in the shop, it is essential to accumulate the gold scrap in every conceivable manner. However, a high rate of return from your refiner is not necessarily good news. Your jewelers may be getting sloppy in their gold use and wasting a lot of inventory.

They may be using excessive amounts of gold and findings for the needed repairs. For example: they may be melting crowns and placing the melted gold in the scrap box. Or when sizing a ring up, using a piece of gold stock much larger than the ring shank. Then filing away the excess gold to fit the shank. This gives your high-grade scrap more material to send to the refiner. However, the gold you are buying in the sizing stock cost the shop more than the amount of money you are getting back from the refiner for the filings.

If your check from the refiner is lower one year, it could be better workmanship and less inventory usage. However, it could be because your jewelers are getting sloppy in taking care of the scrap and not accumulating it properly.

When you compare your returns from year to year, you must also keep in mind the amount of inventory used. Has it gone up or down? Are you satisfied that the maximum efforts are being taken to accumulate all of your scrap? If you are satisfied that these efforts are being made, then the lower rate of return from the refiner is the better news.

Favorite Tips

Always use your lap tray to collect metal filings and save these filings in a container to send to a refiner. Some refiners will supply you with a plastic jar with a screw top lid for these sweeps. Any type of container with a wide mouth top may be used; an old coffee can with a plastic lid works well.

Don't let gold dust walk out of your shop - sweep the floor of the shop daily and mop monthly. Dump the dirty water from mopping in a sink with a gold trap in the drain. Never dump the water in the toilet or other drain without a trap designed to accumulate scrap material.

Place a piece of leather or matte board in the bottom of your lap tray. This will aid you in cleaning the sweeps out of your lap tray. Pick up the leather by the corners and dump the sweeps into the container. This also helps protect stones from the hard metal bottom of the lap tray when accidentally dropped.

Change the filters on your polishing machine regularly. This not only helps profits by accumulating more precious metal dust, but also improves the health of the workers by not having to breathe all the dust and dirt into their lungs. If dust accumulates on the wall near where the air comes out of the dust collector you have waited too long to clean it out and replace the filter.

Precious metal particles are washed down the drain in many shops. To avoid this, install a special precious metal trap in the drain line on the sink in the shop. There are several styles available from tool suppliers. Be certain to purchase one that is made to trap precious metal particles, not just loose stones. For the retail shop, the small drum trap with a separating screen is adequate. Clean this trap out whenever water slows going down the drain.

All broken sawblades should be collected and not thrown away as fine particles of gold are caught in the teeth and can be refined. Also all old emery paper, burs, bristle brushes, rubber abrasive wheels, anything you use to sand, grind, or polish gold needs to be saved with the polishing waste after they are worn out.

Refiners vary greatly in the minimum fees they charge and the rate of return they give. You should contact several refiners, and receive their pricing chart before deciding upon the refiner to use. Find a refiner whose pricing structure fits with the amount of scrap you have to process.

Time spent cleaning the shop is not extra time you need to find. It is time you would spend looking for stones etc. if you did not do the cleaning. It is just spending your time differently. If your bench and shop are organized and you clean it regularly it does not take that much time.

Place a Doormat in the doorway of the shop. Employees can wipe their feet on it as they leave the shop. This will help in removing particles of precious metal off the soles of their shoes. Replace the mat annually and send the old mat to the refiner with the polishing waste.

Workers should always wear an apron in the shop. This keeps gold from filing, grinding, and polishing operations from accumulating in their clothes and being washed down the drain. Thin leather with a tanned smooth surface is best. Cloth aprons, such as denim, are better than nothing, but they will accumulate precious metal down in the fabric. If cloth aprons are used they should not be washed, but sent to the refiner to be burned and the gold recovered.

A shop vacuum cleaner is a necessity. This makes clean up easier, and you will then be more likely to do it more often. This vacuum is for shop use only, and should never be used outside of the shop. Save all bags and send to the refiner with the polishing waste.

If you pay the minimum refining charge you are paying the highest price to have your scrap refined. Always accumulate your scrap long enough to get beyond the minimum charge of the refiner. Never pay a minimum refining charge; if you do, you are paying too much to get your scrap refined.

Do not sell your scrap to a broker who comes into your store, estimates its value, and pays you cash. His margin more than exceeds the money you would save by cheating Uncle Sam on your income taxes.

When accumulating scrap always keep in mind this thought:
WHEN IN DOUBT, DO NOT THROW IT OUT.

'Twas the Month After Christmas

'Twas the month after Christmas, and all through the Shop.
Not a jeweler was stirring, in a chair he had flopped.
The shop is a mess, and the bench is a clutter.
"I can't find a thing," the jeweler had muttered.

When out in the store there arose such a clatter.
He sprung from his bench to see what was the matter.
Away to the front he flew from the shop.
Knocked over his lunch, and spilled soda pop.

Then, what to his wondering eyes should appear?
But from the refiner a container, Oh Dear!
What a wonderful time to clean-up the shop.
Now, where in the world did he put the mop?

More rapid than eagles he flew.
Cleaning the shop was his job to do.
He spoke not a word, but went straight to his chore.
He let no one disturb him by shutting the door.

In all of the dirt that lay on the floor.
Was silver, gold, platinum and more.
The filings, and polishings, and such.
It all has great value, though it don't look like much.

Laying a finger aside of the broom.
He swept up the dirt from the entire room.
To the top of the bench, then on to the wall.
Now sweep away! Sweep away! Sweep away all!

Then on to the polisher, down into its deeps.
He brushed to gather all of the sweeps.

By the time he had finished, from his head to his foot.
His clothes were all dirty with what looked like soot.

The sweeps were all gathered, the job was complete.
The envelopes were filed, everything looked real neat.
The tools were all hung on the bench with care.
When they are needed, he'll know they are there.

The shop is now done, the sweeping concluded.
Organizing the tools was even included.
The gold was all packaged and sent to the refiner.
Now, Profits will increase, Oh what could be finer.

Scrap Management

Date Sent	Place Sent	Type of Material	Weight Sent	Weight Recovered	Time Accumulated

About the Author

Brad Simon is a JA Certified Master Bench Jeweler, and a JA Certified Management Professional. He has worked as a bench jeweler for 26 years, has won over a dozen jewelry design awards, and owns and operates **Simon's Goldsmith Shop**.

Mr. Simon is founder and president of **Bench Media,** publisher of, **E-BENCH** the e-mail newsletter for bench jewelers, **BENCH Magazine,** and **Bench Vision** the multi-media magazine for Bench Jewelers. He and his wife Debbie are co-founders of the Bench Jewelers Conference & Expo.

In addition, Mr. Simon conducts seminars and workshops through **Simon Sez Seminars** on shop management issues and bench techniques and has published two books on jewelry shop management.

Other Books by Brad Simon

Run Your Shop Without It Running You

A Practical Guide To Efficient Shop Management

With over one hundred and fifty pages of information, illustrations, and worksheets, this is the most comprehensive book on Shop Management available today.

Learn a variety of methods to improve profitability of the jewelry shop. Including; how to set correct prices, improve scrap material management, and avoiding costly mistakes at the take-in counter.

Learn methods of increasing productivity without sacrificing quality. Including; organizing and scheduling jobs, shop design, organizing the bench, motivating the bench jeweler, and many other topics.

"For too many years jewelry storeowners have believed the fallacy the shop can't be a profit center. Simon destroys that notion step-by-step with a practical book that shows owners and shop managers the keys to profitability." **Professional Jeweler Magazine**

"All in all, the book is a no-nonsense guide to running a tight repair shop – It's A Must Read." **In-Store Magazine**

"Brad is one of the few people who understand how to make a profit in the shop and how to set prices. If you have a shop or are going to install one, you should buy this book. It's great on setting things up in an orderly fashion for best efficiency, which speeds things up and lowers cost. Buy this book; it's a good one." **David Geller**

"This is going to be one of those classic books that comes to mind whenever someone asks about going into the trade or gets serious about making their shop profitable. There is a lot of practical business sense and many bench tips." **John Caro**

It's About Time

A Bench Jewelers Guide to Increasing Productivity

Proper time management is the key to shop efficiency.

Learn how to organize your work, and schedule your jobs for maximum productivity.

Learn How To Increase Productivity In The Shop Without Sacrificing Quality.

From Fee to Shining Fee

This is the most complete pricing package for jewelry repairs available today. This package consists of a Training Manual and Computer Software.

➤ Learn how to maximize profits in the shop by setting correct prices.

➤ Over two hundred prices arranged in an easy to use two-sheet format.

➤ Easy to follow instructions included.

➤ In minutes you can print out a price list based on your store's information.

➤ Automatically changes prices with changes in Gold, Platinum, or Labor cost.

➤ Completely customizable to fit the needs of your store.

➤ Works equally well for Retail Stores and Trade-Shops.

Bench Media

FOR Bench Jewelers BY Bench Jewelers

Visit These Bench Jewelers websites

BenchBusiness.com

A website devoted to helping Bench Jewelers become more Effective and Efficient.

AboutStoneSetting.com

This website is designed to help jewelers learn and improve their stonesetting skills.

GuideToJewelryMaking.com

Learn how to Make Handmade Jewelry in Silver, Gold, And Platinum from Working Professional Jewelers who are Masters of their Craft.

PlatinumGuru.com

Platinum Guru is a blog on Working with Platinum. Here you will learn all about creating and repairing jewelry made with platinum.

The Bench Jewelers Television Network
BenchTelevision.com

Tips ~ Tricks ~ Tools ~ Techniques ~ Technology
It Is All Here! Everything You Need to Become a Better Bench Jeweler.

The primary purpose of the Bench Jewelers Television Network is to provide TV style How-To Training Videos for Bench Jewelers. Membership to this site allows you unlimited access to all the channels and shows.

**Bench Jewelers Television Network is Produced
BY Bench Jewelers FOR Bench Jewelers
We Know and Understand Your Needs and Concerns**

Each show is filled with high-quality instruction by working jewelers who are masters of their craft.
- From Basic Techniques to Advanced Applications
- From Centuries Old Procedures to the Latest in Technological Advancements
- Each episode provides accurate informative instruction from Professional Bench Jewelers. It is all here for you to view when you want, as often as you want.

"The Bench Jewelers Television Network is exciting! The quality of the work and the level of the expertise are great."
Robyn Hawk

Bench Jewelers Television Network provides a unique learning experience on the Internet for Bench Jewelers. You can access training videos any time day or night 7 days a week from anywhere in the world with broadband access.

Members of the Bench Jewelers Television Network have unlimited access to all of the channels any time of the day or week. You can watch shows over and over as many times as you need. New Episodes air each month and Past Episodes are archived for you to re-watch as often as you like.

"Wow, I can't believe how good the close-up shots are and the quality of video is excellent."
Tom Antion

Each show is filled with high-quality instruction by working jewelers who are masters of their craft and designed to **Inform, Instruct, and Inspire Bench Jewelers** around the world. Whether you are just beginning your career or a seasoned veteran of the bench, you will find extremely valuable information here that will help you become a better bench jeweler. The goal of this site is to provide jewelers with the information and resources they need.

Join Today! BenchTelevision.com

Bench Jewelers Network

BenchJewelersNetwork.com

The Ultimate Website for Bench Jewelers

The Bench Jewelers Network is a Website Community of Professional Bench Jewelers, Students, and Serious Hobbyist. Here you can read articles in our vast library and even watch videos.

We Have It ALL!

Bench Tips	Stone Setting	Laser Welding
Platinum	Pave	Wax Carving
Jewelry	Ring Sizing	Productivity
Pricing	Casting	Channel Setting
Fabrication	Jewelry Making	Shop Safety
Flush Setting	Shop	
Jewelry Repairs	Management	PLUS MORE!

Instructional Articles

All Articles from the Back Issues of Bench Magazine and E-Bench Newsletter PLUS MORE!

Want to learn a new technique, or brush-up on existing skills? Or maybe just curious how other jewelers do their work? Bench Jewelers Network's Article section is all Index by subject and contains everything you want or need to know.

Training Videos

All Episodes from the Bench Jewelers Television Network, Bench Vision DVDs, PLUS MORE!

If a picture is worth a thousand words then a video must be worth MILLIONS! There's nothing like watching a Master perform his work. See how they hold their tools, how they move their hands. Watching how they work is better than reading all the words in the world.

Bench Jewelers Network is produced BY Bench Jewelers FOR Bench Jewelers

We Know and Understand Your Needs and Concerns.

BenchJewelersNetwork.com

www.ingramcontent.com/pod-product-compliance
Lightning Source LLC
Chambersburg PA
CBHW051424170526
45165CB00004BA/1953